M000198428

BOOK ANALYSIS

Written by David Noiret and
Florence Balthasar
Translated by Emma Hanna

The Attack
BY YASMINA KHADRA

Bright
≡Summaries.com

YASMINA KHADRA

ALGERIAN SOLDIER AND WRITER

- **Born in Kenadsa (Algerian Sahara) in 1955.**
- **Notable works:**
  - *The Swallows of Kabul* (2002), novel
  - *The Sirens of Baghdad* (2006), novel
  - *What the Day Owes the Night* (2008), novel

Yasmina Khadra is the pseudonym of Mohammed Moulessehoul, who created the pen-name using his wife's two forenames. Khadra is one of the most influential Algerian authors active today, and writes in French. He was born on 10 January 1955 in Kenadsa, in the Algerian Sahara. Before becoming a novelist, he served as an officer in the Algerian army and participated in the war on terror. He left the army in 2000 to devote himself to writing full-time.

His best-known works include *The Swallows of Kabul* and *The Sirens of Baghdad*, which, along with *The Attack* (2005), form a loosely connected trilogy centred on the tension between the East and the West, as well as *What the Day Owes the Night*, which was adapted into a film in 2012.

THE ATTACK

ON THE FRONT LINES OF THE ISRAELI-PALESTINIAN CONFLICT

- **Genre:** novel
- **Reference edition:** Khadra, Y. (2007) *The Attack*. Cullen, J. Trans. London: Vintage.
- **1ˢᵗ edition:** 2005
- **Themes:** love, violence, hatred, Israeli-Palestinian conflict, religion, multiculturalism

The Attack was first published in French in 2005, and was translated into English the following year. It has won several literary awards, including the Prix des Libraires in 2006. The novel is narrated by Amin, a surgeon working in Tel Aviv, which is being ravaged by the Israeli-Palestinian conflict. In the wake of a suicide bombing in the city centre, he learns that the bomber was none other than his wife, Sihem, who was willing to die for the Palestinian cause. His world is turned upside down, and from that moment onwards, his life is defined by his struggle to understand what could have driven her to commit such a terrible act.

Although this novel draws on a political and cultural reality which continues to divide public opinion around the world even today, it does not take sides in the conflict: instead, it paints a picture of humanity through the lives of the people caught in the middle of it.

SUMMARY

A TERRIBLE SHOCK

The hospital in Tel Aviv is thrown into chaos in the wake of a suicide bombing which has just taken place in a restaurant in the Hakirya district. The attack took a heavy toll: 19 people were killed, and many more were injured. Amin Jaafari, a Palestinian surgeon who is well-integrated in the Jewish community in Israel, carries out emergency surgeries on the survivors throughout the night. When he returns home, Navid Ronnen, a friend who serves in the police force, tells him that he is needed back at the hospital. To his tremendous surprise and horror, he is asked to identify the remains of his wife, Sihem, who is believed to have been the bomber. Amin faints from the shock.

Amin is suspected of being an accomplice, and is taken into custody. He is interrogated by Captain Moshé, but is eventually released thanks to Navid. A few days later, he is beaten up by a group of young Israelis, who accuse him of being a traitor, and his colleague Kim Yehuda allows him to stay with her for a while. Amin is wracked with questions and doubts, and is unable to accept that his wife could have orchestrated the suicide bombing, until he finds a letter in his home which was posted from Bethlehem. In the letter, Sihem begs him for forgiveness. He decides to gather his things and leave for Palestine to look for any sign that he might have previously overlooked which would allow him to understand his wife's motives.

RETRACING SIHEM'S FOOTSTEPS

Kim decides to help Amin as he searches for the truth, and accompanies him as he travels to the cities of Jerusalem and Bethlehem, where Sihem had been staying prior to the attack.

In Bethlehem, Amin is reunited with his foster sister, Leila, and her husband Yasser. They are proud of Sihem's actions, as is everyone else in the city. While he is at their house, Amin notices the cream-coloured Mercedes that a witness claimed to have seen his wife getting into around the time that she had told Amin that she would catch the bus to Kafr Kanna.

Amin pays several visits to the Grand Mosque, where Imam Marwan had blessed Sihem on the night before the attack. However, an armed Islamist group obstructs his attempts to make contact with the imam, as they consider him a traitor – he is not welcome on Palestinian soil, because Israeli forces are searching for him. However, his perseverance eventually pays off, and he is able to speak with the religious leader. The meeting between the two men is tense. Just then, his house in Tel Aviv is vandalised.

Finally, Amin is kidnapped by an Islamic terrorist cell. He is brought before one of their leaders, who says that he is honoured to be in the presence of a suicide bomber's husband. However, their cause goes against everything Amin believes in: while the terrorist leader has chosen a path of violence and destruction, Amin has chosen the path of healing and life.

IN THE HEART OF THE CONFLICT

After this encounter with the terrorist leader, Kim and Amin return to Tel Aviv. Amin goes back home, and begins the long process of putting his house and his thoughts back in order. Suddenly, he remembers something: the last words Sihem ever said to him, which were that she did not like leaving him alone, and that it would be an eternity to her. He then realises that this was her way of telling him that they would never see each other again: it was the sign he had not recognised at the time and had been searching for ever since. Amin looks through a photo album, and sees a photo of his nephew Adel standing beside Sihem, even though he was unaware that they had ever met. Amin's hunger for the truth surges anew, and he decides to continue his investigation by going to Kafr Kanna, where he learns that his wife may have been having an affair with Adel.

Amin tracks Adel to Jenin, the town where he grew up and the site of some of the bloodiest clashes between the Israeli armed forces and Palestinian resistance cells. On the other side of the wall dividing the two communities in the West Bank, he is confronted with the full scale of the horrors of war and learns more about Sihem's actions. She had been planning the attack for a long time, and had even held meetings for advocates of the Palestinian cause in their home.

A WORLD WHERE DEATH IS AN END IN ITSELF

In Jenin, Amin is reunited with his family, including his cousin Jamil, who is able to put him in contact with Adel. Amin is suspected of being a spy for the Shin Bet (the Israeli counterintelligence agency), and is captured and dragged before a group of mujahideen, who soon make him realise how powerless he is and teach him the true meaning of hatred and humiliation. They spend six days tormenting him with the threat of imminent execution, but on the seventh day he is released, as Adel looks on. Adel has rallied to the Islamic cause, and explains how everything started to Amin, as well as reassuring him that he and Sihem never had an affair.

However, the two men's viewpoints are irreconcilable: "I don't fit in the world he's describing. There, death is an end in itself. For a physician, that's too much to swallow" (p. 229). In the end, Amin is taken to Omr, the patriarch of the Jaafari family, by his grandson Wissam. However, this respite is short-lived: Wissam carries out a suicide attack himself, and shortly afterwards,

Israeli bulldozers arrive to raze Omr's house to the ground so that Jewish colonisers can settle there. The entire family is evacuated, and Omr's granddaughter Faten disappears shortly afterwards.

Amin learns that she has been taken to the mosque in Jenin to receive the blessing of Sheikh Marwan, an influential man who commands great respect because of his age and his contacts, who agitates among the Palestinians and encourages them to fight back against Israel instead of standing by passively. Amin goes to Jenin, desperately searching for Faten so that he can prevent yet another suicide bombing. But he is too late: the sermon is interrupted by a drone alert, a missile explodes near the sheikh's car, and Amin is caught in the explosion. As he lies on the verge of death, he has a vision of his younger, happier self. He receives first aid and is taken to hospital, but the medical workers who were dispatched to the scene are unable to save his life.

CHARACTER STUDY

AMIN JAAFARI

Amin Jaafari is the protagonist and narrator of the novel. He lives in Tel Aviv, the capital of Israel, and works as a surgeon. He symbolises the successful integration of a Palestinian in Israel, as he is well-respected in the region and his reputation extends as far as Palestine. Thanks to his job, he is able to live a comfortable, middle-class life, and he owns a magnificent house in one of the poshest districts of Tel Aviv. He has a solid support network consisting of his friend Navid Ronnen, his colleague Kim Sehuda and his boss Ezra Benhaim, with whom he has a close relationship. Meanwhile, another colleague, Ilan Ros, has helped him to find a second home on the coast near Ashkelon. All of this goes to show that Amin was well assimilated into Israeli society before the attack.

As a surgeon, he saves his patients' lives on a daily basis and is good at what he does. In his eyes, human lives are worth more than any cause: "I hate wars and revolutions and these dramas of redemptive violence [...] I'm a surgeon", he says (p. 167).

Amin is the son of a Bedouin and has Arab and Muslim roots. As a non-believer living in the Jewish country of Israel, he finds himself at the crossroads between two nations. He does not have a personal stake in the Israeli-Palestinian conflict until he discovers that his wife has martyred herself in its name. They have been married for 15 years and are non-practicing Muslims, although Sihem does observe Ramadan. He then realises that he had only ever known an idealised version of his wife that existed solely in his mind: "Now that I think about it, how could I have lived her when I never stopped dreaming her?" (p. 184).

Amin has a strong sense of honour, which drives him to search for the truth about his wife. In so doing, he comes into contact with fundamentalists, putting his own life at risk in the process. The novel has a circular narrative, with both the opening and closing scenes describing the apocalyptic carnage that is wrought when Sheikh Marwan's car is blown up. Amin may be a stranger to the conflict, but he ends up on the front lines of the horror engulfing his homeland all the same, and is killed in an Israeli drone strike.

SIHEM

Sihem was Amin's wife until she killed herself in a suicide bombing in Tel Aviv. She does not appear in the novel except through Amin and the other characters' memories and descriptions of her.

The portrait her husband paints of her changes and becomes more contradictory throughout the novel. Although her childhood in Palestine was difficult, Sihem is described as happy, if reserved. Sihem and Amin had a loving relationship: they had a strong bond, travelled together frequently and had a large circle of friends. All in all, they led a happy life in Israel.

However, the suicide bombing reveals that appearances can be deceiving, and Amin discovers a totally different side to his wife's character, which is cast into even sharper relief when he meets Adel, who tells him: "Sihem wasn't so sure she deserved her good fortune [...] She wanted to deserve to live, deserve her reflection in the mirror [...] not just to enjoy her good fortune" (pp. 227-228). He then adds, "Sihem felt closer to her people than she did in your image of her. Maybe she was happy, but not happy enough" (p. 227).

ADEL

Adel is the son of Yasser and Leila, Amin's sister, making him the surgeon's nephew. He calls Amin "Ammu" ("uncle"). Amin believes that his nephew is an honourable, well-intentioned young man until he discovers the truth: that Adel is part of a group of Islamists who are fighting for the Palestinian cause. Adel is in his twenties, and has great respect for Sihem, who "adopted him without a struggle" (p. 128) and gave her life for their shared cause. Amin therefore suspects him of having had an affair with his wife, but Adel categorically denies this accusation.

Amin does not meet Adel until he is kidnapped by terrorists near the end of the novel. Their confrontation, which was the end goal of all of Amin's travels through Palestinian territory, is the emotional crux of the novel. The reader discovers that Adel and his uncle hold completely opposing worldviews: the former is devoted to the fight for his people's freedom, while the latter believes that individual lives are worth more than any cause. He rejects Adel's world, where "death is an end in itself" (p. 229). The two men are unable to find common ground, and their encounter ends in disappointment and estrangement.

KIM SEHUDA

Kim Sehuda is a colleague, fellow surgeon and old friend of Amin's whom he met during their time at university. She is "beautiful and spontaneous and far more open-minded than the other students, who had to bite their tongues a few times before they'd ask an Arab for a light, even if he was a brilliant student and a handsome lad to boot" (p. 9). They had flirted briefly during their university days, but Kim had met a Russian man and fallen hopelessly in love with him. He then left her without any warning to return to his own country.

Those flirtations eventually turned into a strong friendship. The day after Amin's life is turned upside down, Kim takes him under her wing: she lets him stay with her, tries to reason with him, looks after him after he is attacked and ends up accompanying him on his travels in spite of his fits of anger and the dangerousness of his quest. She takes Amin to the coast to visit her grandfather as a respite from the turmoil of Tel Aviv, and also stays by his side during his reckless trip to Bethlehem. After their first journey retracing Sihem's footsteps, she steps back, leaving Amin alone, and disappears during the final section of the novel.

All in all, Kim is a loyal, devoted friend with "a generous heart" (p. 9), who accompanies Amin in his investigations for as long as she is able.

NAVID RONNEN

Navid Ronnen is a senior official in the Tel Aviv police force. His cheerful disposition and sense of humour make him one of Amin's "most engaging patients" (p. 26). After Amin performed a successful operation on Navid's mother, their relationship blossomed into a true friendship.

Navid is of Israeli origin and is well aware of the reality of the situation in his homeland. Through his job, he comes into regular contact with "a lot of criminals [...] and a lot of plain psychopaths" (p. 92), including terrorists. Like Kim, Navid is always willing to help Amin, despite the latter's temper and mistrust – in fact, Navid rescues him on two separate occasions, and he is not the only one to do so. When Amin falls apart upon learning what Sihem has done, Navid talks about his own inability to understand her motivations:

> "How the hell is it possible for an ordinary human being, sound in body and mind, to make that choice? Does he have a fantasy or a hallucination that convinces him he's been given a divine mission? How can he give up his plans, his dreams, his ambitions, and decide to die an atrocious death in the midst of the worst kind of barbarism?" (p. 93)

Navid helps Amin to cross the border into Palestine for his final journey, despite his position in the police force.

FATEN

Faten Jaafari is the granddaughter of Omr, the family patriarch, and is described as "a sturdy, uncouth young woman, formed by a lifetime of demanding household tasks and the austere existence of the enclaved villages" (p. 237).

She is 35 years old, and has "had more than her share of misfortune" (p. 237), as her first husband was killed immediately after their wedding and her second fiancé died days before theirs. Since then, she has devoted her life to taking care of Omr: "Without her, Omr wouldn't make it. In the beginning, other members of the family agreed to take care of him, but he wound up neglected" (pp. 249-250).

She was already hostile towards the Israelis, believing that they "have no more heart than their [bulldozers]" (p. 248), but when her grandfather's house is destroyed, this hostility calcifies into outright hatred. The next day, she has vanished without a trace, having left to fight for the Palestinian cause. Amin realises that Faten has left her family to become a martyr, and sets off to look for her in Jenin, where he is killed in an attack on the town mosque.

ANALYSIS

HISTORICAL AND POLITICAL CONTEXT

The story is set in a climate of constant tension between Jews and Arabs, "two chosen peoples who have elected to turn a land blessed by God into a field of horror and rage" (p. 166), as shown by the reaction of a Jewish man who was injured in the attack and who refuses to be treated by Amin because he is Palestinian.

Key dates in the Israeli-Palestinian conflict

- Towards the end of the 19th century, Palestine was under Ottoman occupation. Its inhabitants were 85% Muslim, 10% Christian and 5% Jewish.
- Following the First World War (1914-1918), the country was placed under British mandate.
- During the Second World War (1939-1945), anti-Semitism in the form of pogroms and then the Holocaust – referenced in the novel

by Kim's grandfather – gave rise to Zionism, a movement which advocated the creation of a Jewish state. Thousands of concentration camp survivors immigrated to Palestine to create a national homeland there.

- In the 1930s, the first Palestinian rebellions broke out and were repressed by the occupying British forces.
- In 1947, Britain withdrew from the conflict, and the UN, which was created after the Second World War, voted in favour of dividing Palestine into two separate nations: one Jewish, the other Arab. Meanwhile, Jerusalem was declared international territory, as a city with large Christian, Jewish and Muslim populations alike "with its minarets and its church towers" (p. 141).
- Israel declared its independence on 14 May 1948. It shared borders with Egypt and the Gaza Strip to the south-west, with Jordan and the West Bank to the east, with Lebanon to the north and with Syria to the north-east.
- In 1949, Israel became a member of the UN. At that point, Gaza and the West Bank were under Arab control. Since neither side was satisfied with the UN's plan to divide the country, a

civil war broke out, and soon escalated into an international war.

- In 1964, the Palestine Liberation Organization (PLO) was created, and Yasser Arafat (Palestinian statesman, 1929-2004) was named chairman in 1969. He became the president of the Palestinian National Authority in 1996.

- In 1993, the Oslo Accords envisioned the establishment of an independent Palestinian state.

- In 2002, a security barrier was installed along the length of the West Bank border, shielding approximately 15% of the Jewish colonies there. The stated purpose of this wall is to prevent Palestinian terrorist attacks, and it is mentioned in the novel on several occasions:

> "Nevertheless, I have seen many things since I passed to the other side of the Wall: small villages in the state of siege; checkpoints on every access road; larger roads littered with charred vehicles blasted by drones; cohorts of the damned, lined up and waiting their turn to be checked, pushed about, and often turned back." (p. 200)

Historical references in the novel

This novel is far from being a work of pure fiction, and is grounded in historical fact, providing the reader with ample food for thought about the Israeli-Palestinian conflict. The story echoes historical reality by mentioning individuals and movements which directly influenced and shaped the course of the war.

As such, Amin's story is anchored in a very specific context and could realistically have taken place during the Second Intifada (2000-2004). The Intifada, which is an Arabic word meaning "tremor" when translated literally, refers to a Palestinian rebellion against the Israeli occupation. This conflict has also been called the "stone war", a name which is evoked when the children stone Israeli cars.

There were two major groups involved in this revolt: the Islamic Jihad, a nationalist group which key member states of the UN consider to be a terrorist organisation, and Hamas, an Islamist movement which consists of a political wing and a paramilitary wing, is mainly active in Gaza and aims to eliminate the State of Israel.

Other organisations working towards the goal of Palestinian independence were also involved, and *The Attack* focuses on the operations of the al-Aqsa Martyrs' Brigades, which is one of the militias that support the Fatah faction, a Palestinian political and military movement founded in 1959 by Yasser Arafat.

The novel also references one of the most influential figures in the history of Israel: Ariel Sharon (Israeli general and politician, 1928-2014), who was considered the Israeli army's most effective commander. He also served as Prime Minister of Israel from 2001 to 2006 as part of a right-wing government.

The Shin Bet, the Israeli counterintelligence agency, also known as Shabak, also plays a role in the novel's plot. Members of the terrorist groups actually accuse Amin of acting on the agency's orders, as it works to detect and prevent any attacks on Israeli soil.

A POLYPHONIC NARRATIVE

Multiple points of view

One of the main risks associated with writing a novel about such a contentious topic is to unintentionally or unconsciously get too close to the subject matter and start taking sides. However, Khadra sidesteps this trap by using multiple points of view. Amin's journey takes him through both Israel and Palestine, and he encounters a wide variety of people involved in the conflict along the way, as well as their different reactions to it:

- **Ignorance**. Before he was personally affected, Amin was one of the people who was ignorant of the conflict, or more accurately, who turned a blind eye to "the traumatic events that undermined hopes for reconciliation between two chosen peoples who have elected to turn a land blessed by God into a field of horror and rage" (p. 166). Initially, the surgeon represents a section of the population which is not necessarily indifferent to the conflict, but which does not have a personal stake in it. Instead, he remains on the outside, not "applauding the combatants on one side or condemning the combatants on the other [because] they all share an attitude [he] find[s] senseless and depressing" (*ibid.*). These people are simply trying to live their lives, or at the very least, to survive. However, Amin is not entirely passive: "Instead of turning the other cheek or fighting back, I chose to care for patients" (*ibid.*).

- **Distrust and racism**. Decades of bloody conflict have created a climate where distrust and racism reign supreme. Amin has regularly had to face racism during his time in Israel, from his university days to the present: "All too aware of the stereotypes that mark me out in the public square, I strive to overcome them, one by one, by doing the best I can do and putting up with the incivilities of my Jewish comrades" (pp. 96-97). For example, Ilan Ros has never trusted Amin because of his origins, and therefore harbours a great deal of jealousy towards him. After the attack, this paranoia only increases: Amin is detained by the police on several occasions, and is even harassed by young Israelis in his own home, while also being suspected of acting under orders from the Israeli secret services during

his time in Palestine.
- **Individual trust**. In spite of the brutal conflict, some characters are able to look beyond generalisations and prejudices and judge each individual on their own merits by considering them as independent beings who deserve to be given the benefit of the doubt, no matter what everyone else thinks of them. For Amin, these people can be divided into two major groups: his friends (Kim, Navid, Ezra Benhaim and the glazier) and his patients. He is very dear to his friends: Ezra Benhaim, the hospital director, supported Amin right from the start "to keep [his] detractors at bay" (p. 7). Amin's Bedouin roots do not matter to him, as his worth is proven by his prowess as a surgeon. Meanwhile, Amin's patients see him as the surgeon who treated them and, in some cases, who saved their lives: his skilful work allows them to bypass any racist prejudices they may be harbouring and to judge him on his capabilities rather than his origins. In fact, when Ilan Ros starts a wildly popular petition to bar Amin from returning to the hospital, many of his former patients protest against it. This leaves the hospital backed into a corner,

caught between the signatories on one side and Amin's former patients on the other.

- **Passive engagement**. Another large chunk of the population falls into this category, in which an individual sides with their respective homeland: for example, an Israeli citizen might be overheard saying "The Palestinians refuse to listen to reason" (p. 64). Meanwhile, many Palestinians tell Amin that they are proud of Sihem's sacrifice, including Yasser and his wife Leila, Amin's foster sister, and their son confides in Amin that "They're militants, too, in their way" (p. 226). However, taking this nationalist stance does not necessarily translate to action.

- **Active, often violent engagement**. For certain individuals, their commitment to the cause is very real and is based on action. They often belong to organisations such as the Islamic Jihad, the Hamas or the al-Aqsa Martyrs' Brigades, opposed by the police and the Israeli secret services. The two sides have been caught in a game of cat and mouse for many years, and the resulting violence is inescapable. For example, when Sheikh Marwan calls on the Palestinians to join the cause and fight, the Israeli secret services launch an attack on the service he is conducting. The commander Amin meets near Jenin explains how he views the problem:

> "The problem, Doctor, is that other people deny [young Palestinians] those dreams. Other people are trying to confine them to ghettos until they're trapped in them for good. And that's the reason why they prefer to die. When dreams are turned away, death becomes the ultimate salvation." (p. 220)

Adel, Sihem and Wissam are committed to the Palestinian cause, and the latter two go as far as to sacrifice their lives for it.

There is a thin line between passive and active engagement, as exemplified by the character of Faten: she lives a relatively tranquil life in a Palestinian village, but she is driven to make the leap from passive to active engagement when her home is destroyed in Israeli reprisals.

Introspection

Amin's quest for the truth reveals him to be a profoundly humanist man who supports a message of peace and tolerance. Other characters, Israelis and Palestinians alike, also reflect on the senselessness of the conflict, which Navid describes as follows:

> "As soon as we collect our dead, our leaders send up the copters to smoke a few Arab hovels. Then, just when the government is getting ready to declare victory, a fresh attack sets the clock back. How long can it go on?" (p. 64)

When Amin crosses the border into the West Bank, he meets Zeev, a hermit with whom he speaks at length. One particular truth emerges from their conversations: "Every Jew in Palestine is a bit of an Arab, and no Arab in Israel can deny that he's a little Jewish. [...] So why so much hate between relatives?" (p. 242).

The novel explores a variety of attitudes on both the Israeli and Palestinian sides. Mired in a conflict with no prospect of resolution in sight, both sides perpetuate an endless cycle of violence without ever looking at the big picture, and by considering a variety of perspectives, the novel casts their shared intransigence in stark relief. It also highlights something else that the two peoples have in common: the countless victims who have perished on both sides. The novel's polyphonic approach therefore gives the reader significant food for thought.

THE FORM

Stylistic techniques

The novel uses a circular narrative, wherein the opening and closing scenes are one and the same: the narrator being caught up in the ensuing explosion when Sheikh Marwan's car is targeted in an attack. This is a way of surprising the reader, as the novel will give them a certain feeling of déjà vu when they reach its closing pages, as well as reminding them of how it all began. This is also the author's way of showing that the story ends where it begins, and is therefore a self-contained entity.

However, this novel adds another dimension to this technique by surprising the reader in a second way, as they will be led to believe that the first explosion is the one alluded to in the title. However, the titular attack does not actually take place until the following chapter, which will take the reader by surprise and force them to revise their initial expectations. This means that the title could be considered to have multiple, equally valid meanings.

In fact, the first pages of the novel depict the end of the story, when the narrator, Amin Jaafari, is accidentally killed. This narrative technique is known as a flashforward, or prolepsis, and involves the depiction of events which do not actually take place until much later in the story. In this case, the following chapters take place before Amin's death, and follow the last weeks of his life as he learns of the first attack, discovers his wife's involvement and begins his investigation.

From a thematic perspective, the purpose of emphasising this single event is twofold:

- **Repetition**. The explosions and the Israeli drone strikes are repeated, giving the impression that the attacks will never end on either side of the wall.
- **Echo**. The final explosion echoes the attack caused by Sihem at the start of the novel. Both peoples are directly confronted with the horrors of the civil war. The pain and suffering

borne by the Israelis and the Palestinians also echo each other: when one side is dealt a blow, it will not be long before the other side will have to face the reprisals.

The novel is written in the first person, allowing it to focus more fully on one man's personal quest in the midst of a complex geopolitical conflict. Amin is therefore a first-hand witness to the events he describes, and the novel ends with his death. The last lines of the book seem to be his final thoughts, as he thinks back on something his father once told him: "They can take everything you own – your property, your best years, all your joys, all your good works, everything down to your last shirt – but you'll always have your dreams, so you can reinvent your stolen world" (p. 257).

Internal monologue

The use of internal monologue plunges the reader into the depths of the main character's mind. By giving us unrestricted access to his innermost thoughts, boundaries become hazy: words blur into thoughts and thoughts into words. This brings us closer to the main character and gives us a deeper understanding of him.

The novel's syntax is also used to further emphasise the lack of distinction between narrator and character. The narrative often takes the form of a stream of consciousness, which is characterised by shorter sentences and follows Amin's train of thought even when it suddenly turns in a different direction: "It was in this exact spot that my mother buried my stillborn puppy. My grief was so great that she wept along with me. My mother... a charitable soul [...]" (p. 239).

Furthermore, the internal monologue is often used to address specific themes such as questioning, struggling with one's own identity, the search for the truth, doubt, theorising, and so on. Amin's mind is inundated with doubts, incomprehension and denial, which renders him by turns speechless, distraught and driven to frantic action. For example, when Amin reads Sihem's letter, he says "My last reference points have hit the fucking road" (p. 70).

This stylistic choice allows us to follow Amin's "painful search for the truth [that] has been [his] personal voyage of initiation" (p. 233) first-hand, bearing witness to all his worries, doubts and progress. The reader therefore has all the information they need to understand his journey, his realisations and his character development.

Poetic language

The novel is saturated with metaphors, and the language used throughout is reminiscent of poetry. This stylistic choice juxtaposes the novel's form with its content, given that its themes of terrorism and deadly violence are dark, tragic and ultimately prosaic. This technique echoes the contrast between the protagonist's pacifism and devotion to humanity, and the Palestinians' suicide bombings and the targeted Israeli attacks. This contrast produces strikingly beautiful prose:

> "Night is preparing to strike camp as the dawn grows impatient at the gates of the city. [...] No trace of romance remains in the sky, no cloud proposes to temper the fiery zeal of the newborn sun. Even if its light were supposed to be Revelation itself, it would not warm my soul." (pp. 34-35)

Khadra's writing style allows the reader to feel

the intermingled pain and beauty experienced by the characters almost as their own. He also uses a number of metaphors involving the sea ("Away out on the water, an ocean liner twinkles. Closer in, the waves hurl themselves desperately against the rocks. Their racket resounds in my head like the blows of a club," p. 52), resulting in a romantic writing style which links natural imagery with human emotions. This poetic style creates a kind of shield against the bloody realities of war. Khadra has also stated that he wrote *The Attack* "to denounce the absurdity of this war, to make people aware of this human tragedy and of the injustices it is spawning, to highlight the inconsistency of the ideologies that are crushing spirits and transforming the powerful into persecutors. Because there is nothing more important than an individual's life, no doctrine, no ideology, no cause which takes precedence over the right to life. Furthermore, nothing on Earth belongs to us, including our homelands and our heritage, because the only riches we can legitimately claim are our own lives." (Urquiza, 2012)[1]. In this way, Khadra does take a stance, not for or against

---

1. This quotation has been translated by BrightSummaries.com.

either side, but against the very nature of war
itself.

FURTHER REFLECTION

SOME QUESTIONS TO THINK ABOUT...

- In your opinion, what is the message of *The Attack*? Which character is used to deliver it?
- What is your interpretation of the novel's title?
- Explain Amin's relationship with his heritage. Does he come into conflict with it?
- "Instead of turning the other cheek or fighting back, I chose to care for patients" (p. 166). Use this quote, which is uttered by Amin, to analyse how much importance the novel places on individual lives, in comparison to the importance it places on fighting for a "bigger" cause such as a nation's freedom.
- Compare the message of *The Attack* and the following quote from Albert Camus (French author, 1913-1960) regarding the Algerian War (1954-1962) during his Nobel Prize acceptance speech: "People are now planting bombs in the tramways of Algiers. My mother might be on one of those tramways. If that is justice,

then I prefer my mother" (Blincoe, 2013).

- Amin places more value on his love for his wife than on a war fought in the name of a "higher" cause. Is this a selfish attitude? Justify and expand your answer by considering the ways love is addressed in the novel.
- Is it possible to be simultaneously neutral and engaged, like Amin, in any situation? Explain your answer.
- Compare the situation in Tel Aviv with the situations in Jerusalem, Bethlehem and Jenin.
- Certain aspects of *The Attack* are typical of noir fiction. To what extent does the book fall into this literary genre? Explain your answer.
- After watching the film, compare its narrative structure with that of the novel. What perspective did the director adopt? In your opinion, was it a successful adaptation?

We want to hear from you!
Leave a comment on your online library
and share your favourite books on social media!

FURTHER READING

REFERENCE EDITION

- Khadra, Y. (2007) *The Attack*. Cullen, J. Trans. London: Vintage.

REFERENCE STUDIES

- Blincoe, N. (2013) Camus and the Algerian Revolution. *Asharq al-Awsat*. [Online]. [Accessed 18 December 2017]. Available from: <https://eng-archive.aawsat.com/nicholas-blincoe2/lifestyle-culture/jennacamus-and-the-algerian-revolution>

- Urquiza, L. (2012) Le romancier Yasmina Khadra répond à vos questions. *The World Bank*. [Online]. [Accessed 18 December 2017]. Available from: <http://blogs.worldbank.org/youthink/fr/le-romancier-yasmina-khadra-r-pond-vos-questions>

ADAPTATIONS

- Dauvillier, L. and Chapron, G. (2016) *The Attack*. [Graphic novel]. Ontario: Firefly.

- *The Attack*. (2013) [Film]. Ziad Doueiri. Dir. France/

Belgium/Qatar/Egypt: Canal+.

MORE FROM
BRIGHTSUMMARIES.COM

- Reading guide – *The Swallows of Kabul* by Yasmina Khadra.
- Reading guide – *What the Day Owes the Night* by Yasmina Khadra.

www.brightsummaries.com

Ebook EAN: 9782808007290

Paperback EAN: 9782808007771

Legal Deposit: D/2017/12603/969

This guide was written with the collaboration of
Florence Balthasar for the analysis of the characters
Kim Sehuda, Navid Ronnen, Faten and Sihem, and for
the chapters "A polyphonic narrative" and "Internal
monologue".

Cover: © Primento

Digital conception by Primento, the digital partner of
publishers.

Made in the USA
Coppell, TX
16 March 2022

75057235R00036